ACKNOWLEDGMENTS

Publishing Director	Piers Pickard
Publisher	Tim Cook
Commissioning Editor	Jen Feroze
Illustrators	Andy Mansfield
	Sebastien Iwohn
Designer	Andy Mansfield
Print production	Larissa Frost,
	Nigel Longuet

With thanks to: Jennifer Dixon

Published in March 2017 by Lonely Planet Global Ltd
CRN: 554153
ISBN: 978 1 78657 317 9
www.lonelyplanetkids.com
© Lonely Planet 2017
Printed in China

10 9 8 7 6 5 4 3 2 1

Lonely Planet Offices

AUSTRALIA
The Malt Store, Level 3, 551 Swanston St, Carlton, Victoria 3053
T: 03 8379 8000

IRELAND
Unit E, Digital Court, The Digital Hub,
Rainsford St, Dublin 8

USA
124 Linden St, Oakland, CA 94607
T: 510 250 6400

UK
240 Blackfriars Rd, London SE1 8NW
T: 020 3771 5100

STAY IN TOUCH lonelyplanet.com/contact

first words
SPANISH

TAXI

Illustrated by
Andy Mansfield & Sebastien Iwohn

hello

---

hola

(oh-lah)

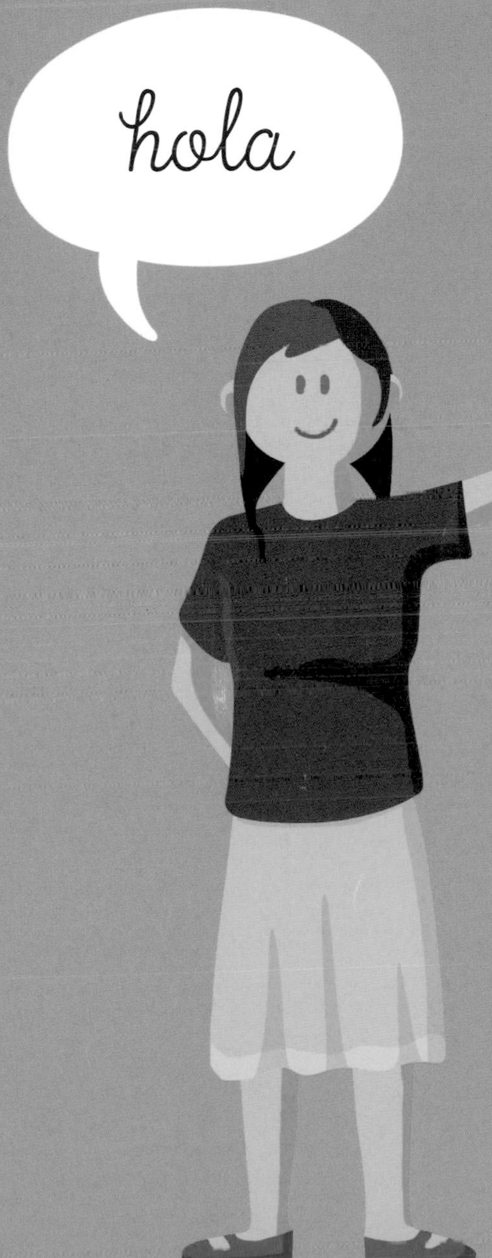
hola

ice cream
helado
(eh-lah-doh)

water

---

agua

(a-gwa)

supermarket

supermercado

(soo-pair-mair-kah-doh)

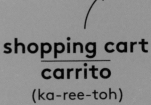

shopping cart
carrito
(ka-ree-toh)

cat

---

gato

(ga-toh)

bus

autobús

(ow-toh-boos)

dress

---

vestido

(ves-tee-doh)

dog

perro

(peh-roh)

banana
---
plátano
(pla-ta-noh)

carrot

zanahoria

(za-na-or-ree-ya)

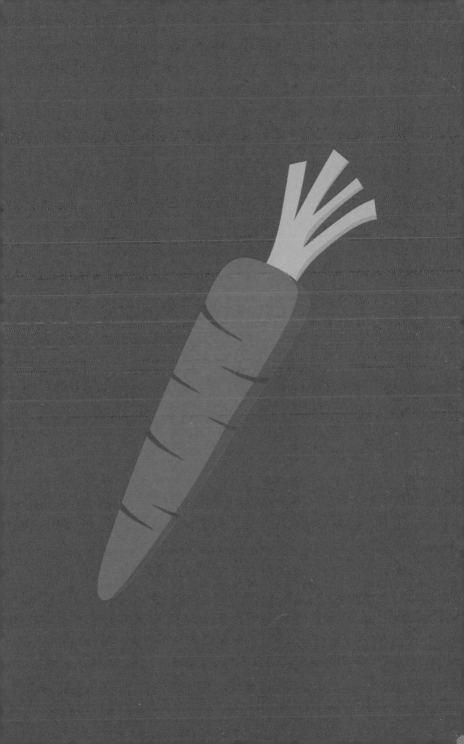

$$\frac{taxi}{taxi}$$

(tak-see)

t-shirt

---

camiseta

(ka-mee-seh-ta)

fish

---

pescado

(pes-kah-doh)

airplane

avión

(av-ee-on)

horse
___
caballo
(ka-ba-yo)

french fries
patatas fritas
(pa-ta-tas free-tas)

swimming pool
piscina
(pee-see-na)

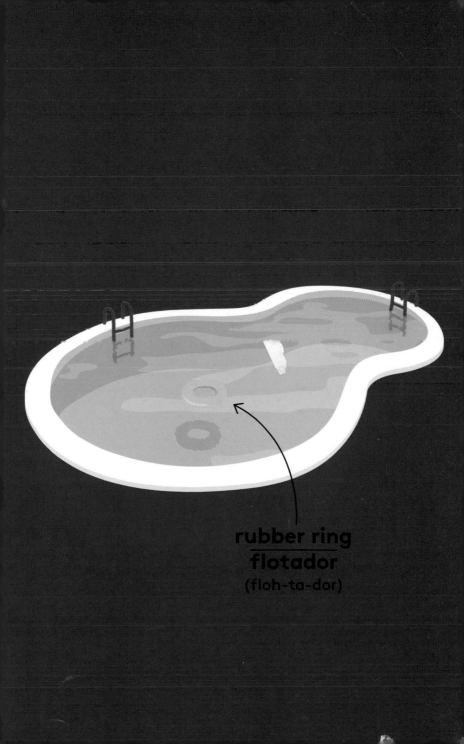

rubber ring
flotador
(floh-ta-dor)

cheese
---
queso

(keh-soh)

towel

toalla

(toh-al-ya)

doctor

doctor/doctora

(dok-tor/dok-tora)

apple

manzana

(man-za-na)

worm

gusano
(goo-sa-noh)

beach
---
playa

(pla-ya)

bicycle
bicicleta
(bee-see-kle-ta)

airport

aeropuerto

(aye-roh-pwair-toh)

juice

---

jugo

(khoo-go)

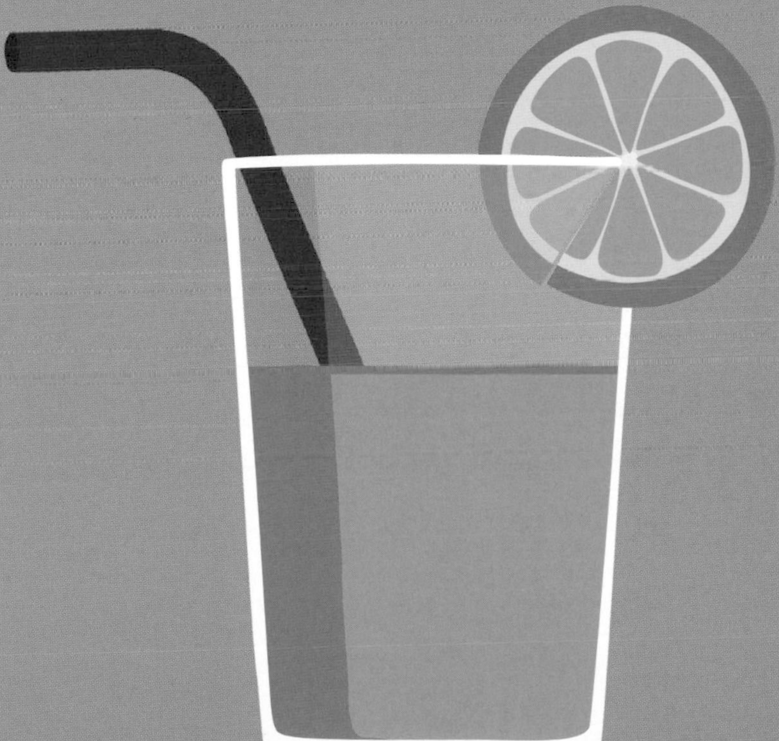

bakery

---

panadería

(pa-na-de-ree-a)

panadería

shoes
---
zapatos

(za-pa-tos)

phone
teléfono
(te-leh-foh-noh)

post office

---

correos

(ko-ray-os)

restaurant
restaurante
(res-tow-ran-teh)

hotel
hotel
(oh-tel)

milk
---
leche

(leh-tchay)

chocolate
chocolate
(tcho-koh-lah-teh)

car
---
coche

(ko-tchay)

hat
---
sombrero

(som-brair-roh)

sunglasses

gafas de sol

(ga-fas dey sol)

chicken
pollo
(pol-yo)

train
---
tren

(tren)

station
estación
(es-ta-see-on)

clock
reloj
(re-lokh)

toilet
---
servicio

(sair-vee-see-oh)

bed
---
cama

(ka-ma)

house

---

casa

(ka-sa)

chimney
chimenea
(tchi-me-nay-a)

pants

pantalones

(pan-ta-loh-nes)

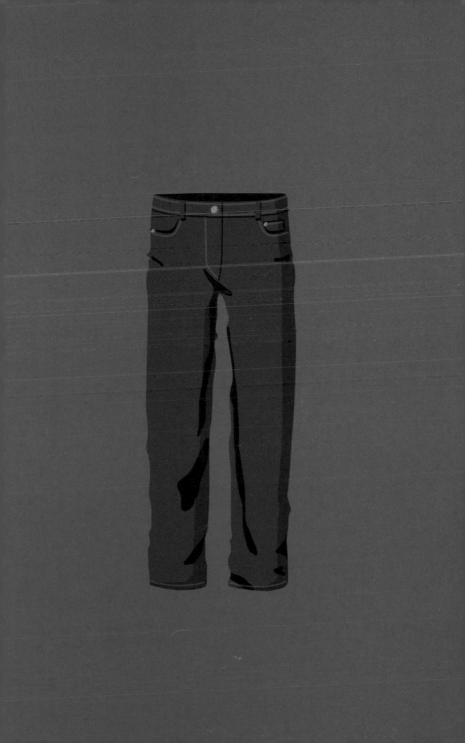

suitcase
maleta
(ma-leh-ta)

plate
plato

(pla-toh)

knife

---

cuchillo

(koo-tchee-lyo)

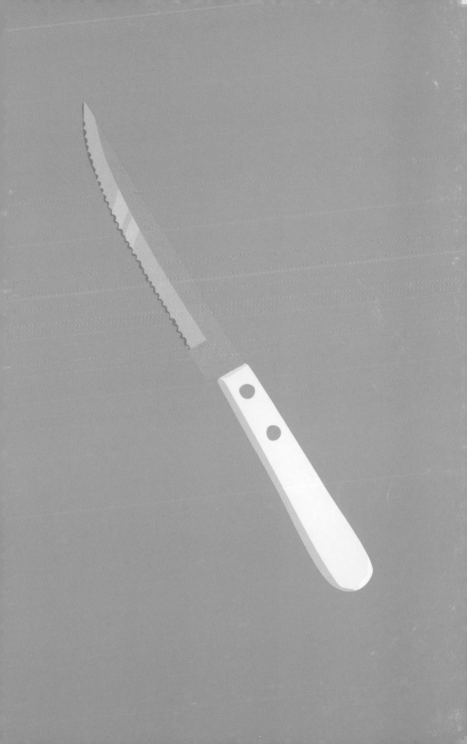

fork
---
tenedor

(teh-nay-dor)

spoon
cuchara
(koo-tcha-ra)

computer

---

ordenador

(or-day-na-dor)

mouse
ratón
(ra-ton)

book
libro
(lee-broh)

sandwich

emparedado

(em-pa-reh-dah-doh)

yes

sí

(see)

no
---
no

(no)

movie theater
cine
(see-nay)

park

---

parque

(par-keh)

menu

menú

(meh-noo)

El Menú

passport

pasaporte

(pas-a-por-teh)

police officer
policía
(po-lee-see-a)

key
llave
(lya-vay)

ticket
boleto

(bo-leh-toh)

pineapple
piña

(pee-nya)

rain
lluvia

(lyoo-vee-ah)

snow
---
nieve
(nee-eh-vay)

sun
---
sol

(sol)

tree

árbol

(ahr-bol)

flower

flor

(flor)

cake

---

pastel

(pas-tel)

cherry
cereza
(seh-reh-sa)

ball
---
pelota

(peh-lo-ta)

bird

---

pájaro

(pa-kha-roh)

egg

huevo

(way-voh)

umbrella

---

paraguas

(pa-ra-gwas)

rabbit

---

conejo

(ko-neh-khoh)

money
dinero

(dee-nair-roh)

bank

---

banco

(ban-koh)

mouse

---

ratón

(ra-ton)

scarf

---

bufanda

(boo-fan-da)

gloves
guantes
(gwan-tes)

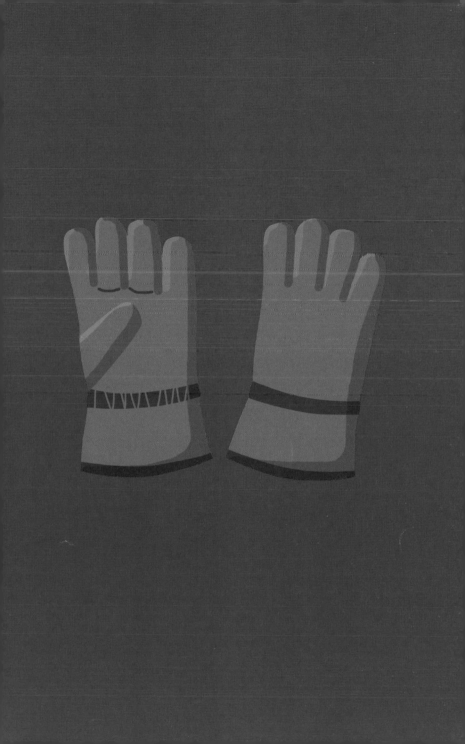

coat

---

abrigo

(a-bree-goh)

hospital
hospital
(os-pee-tal)

chair
silla

(see-lya)

table
---
mesa

(meh-sa)

toothbrush
cepillo de dientes
(theh-pee-lyo dey dyen-tes)

toothpaste
dentífrico
(den-tee-free-koh)

sunscreen

crema solar

(kray-ma so-lar)

spf 50

lion

---

león

(lay-on)

elephant
elefante
(eh-lay-fan-tay)

monkey

---

mono

(mo-noh)

spider
---
araña
(a-ra-nya)

burger
hamburguesa
(am-boor-gay-sa)

pen
bolígrafo
(boh-lee-gra-foh)

door

puerta

(pwair-ta)

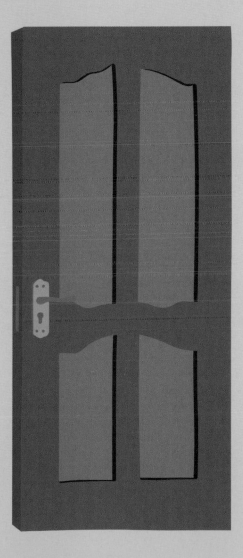

window

---

ventana

(ven-ta-na)

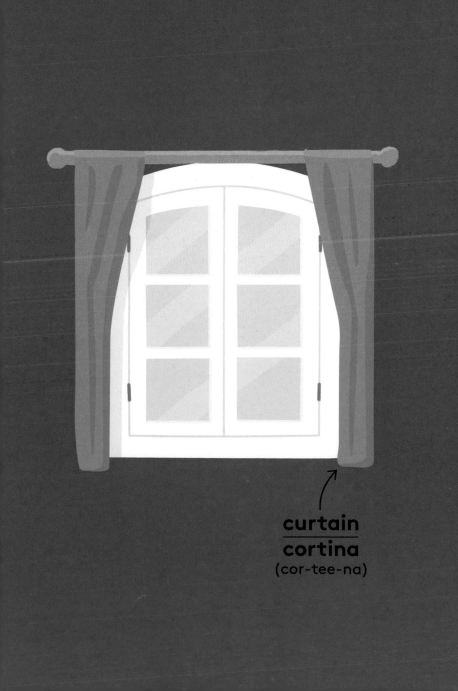

curtain
cortina
(cor-tee-na)

tent
tienda

(tee-en-da)

church
iglesia
(ee-glay-see-ah)

tomato
---
tomate

(tom-ah-tay)

moon
___
luna

(loo-na)

stars
estrellas

(es-tray-yas)

postcard

postal

(pos-tal)

stamp

sello

(say-yo)

boat

---

barco

(bar-koh)

goodbye
adiós

(a-dee-oss)